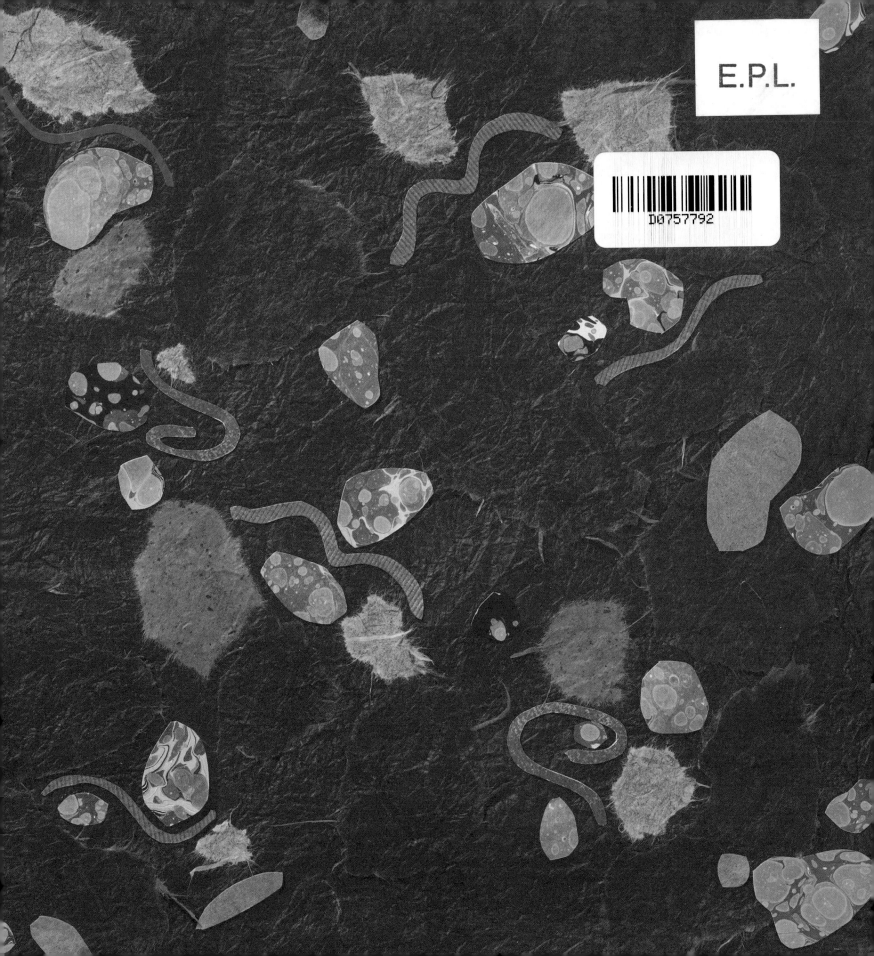

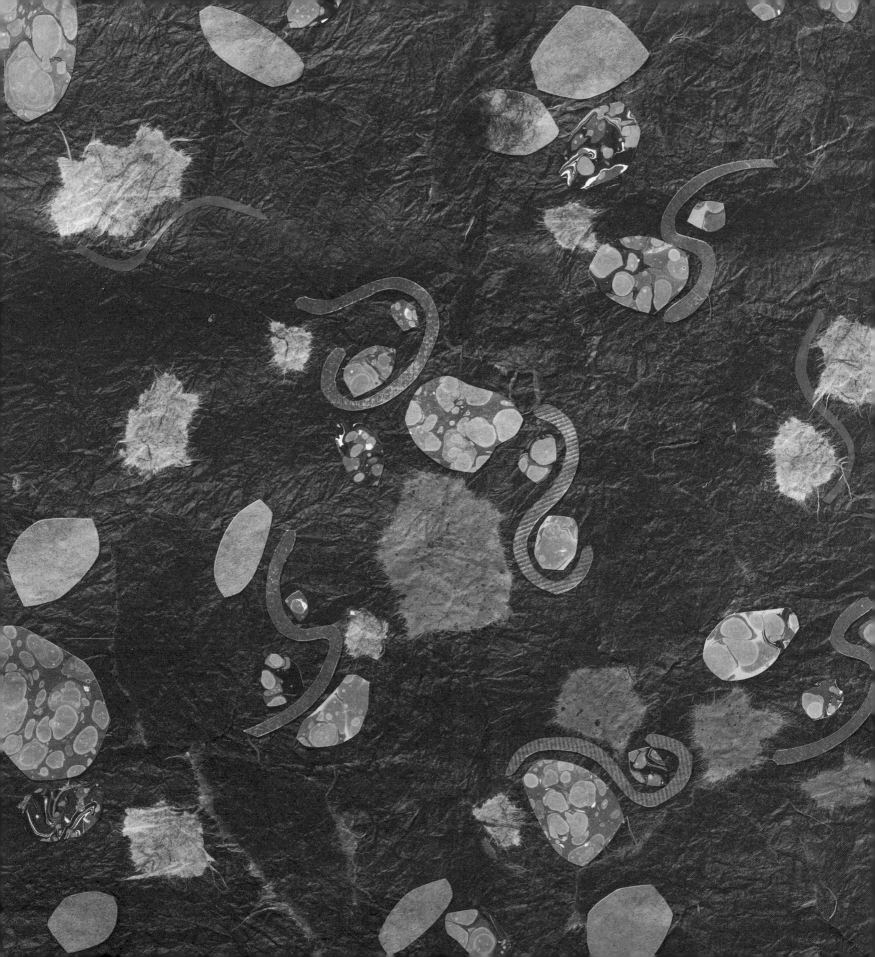

# Compost Stew

## An A to Z Recipe for the Earth

With love and thanks to my mother, who started the first batch,
and to my husband, Owen, who keeps it going.  —MMS

For Nina "MooMoo" Moore, who loved me and her garden,
and for Lucy, who helps me herd all my red wigglers.  —AW

AUTHOR'S NOTE

When plants, animals, and minerals break down, they are returned to the earth to become part of the soil. That's what happens with compost. Laundry lint, for example, which is made up of cotton fiber from your clothes, quickly breaks down in the compost. Quarry dust, which is finely ground rock powder, adds minerals that improve the soil. And when worms eat their way through the compost, it comes out the other end as castings that further enrich the soil and help plants to grow. To learn more about composting, including how to start your own home compost heap, visit http://aggie-horticulture.tamu.edu/sustainable/slidesets/kidscompost/cover.html.

Text copyright © 2010 by Mary McKenna Siddals
Illustrations copyright © 2010 by Ashley Wolff

All rights reserved.
Published in the United States by Tricycle Press, an imprint of the Crown Publishing Group, a division of Random House, Inc., New York.
www.crownpublishing.com
www.tricyclepress.com

Tricycle Press and the Tricycle Press colophon are registered trademarks of Random House, Inc.

Library of Congress Cataloging-in-Publication Data
Siddals, Mary McKenna.
  Compost stew : an A to Z recipe for the earth / by Mary McKenna Siddals ; illustrations by Ashley Wolff. — 1st ed.
      p. cm.
  Summary: A rhyming recipe explains how to make the dark, crumbly, rich, earth-friendly food called compost.
[1. Stories in rhyme. 2. Compost—Fiction.]  I. Wolff, Ashley, ill. II. Title.
  PZ8.3.S5715Co 2010
  [E—dc22
                                2009016300

ISBN 978-1-58246-316-2 (hardcover)
ISBN 978-1-58246-341-4 (Gibraltar lib. bdg.)

Printed in China

Design by Chloe Rawlins
Typeset in Soft Compound and Adobe Jenson Pro
The illustrations in this book were rendered using gouache and collage.

1 2 3 4 5 6 – 15 14 13 12 11 10

First Edition

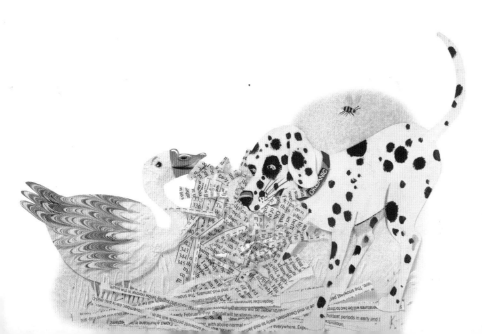

# Compost Stew

## An A to Z Recipe for the Earth

by Mary McKenna Siddals

Illustrated by Ashley Wolff

TRICYCLE PRESS
Berkeley

Environmental chefs,
here's a recipe for you
to fix from scratch
to mix a batch
of Compost Stew.

Ingredients:

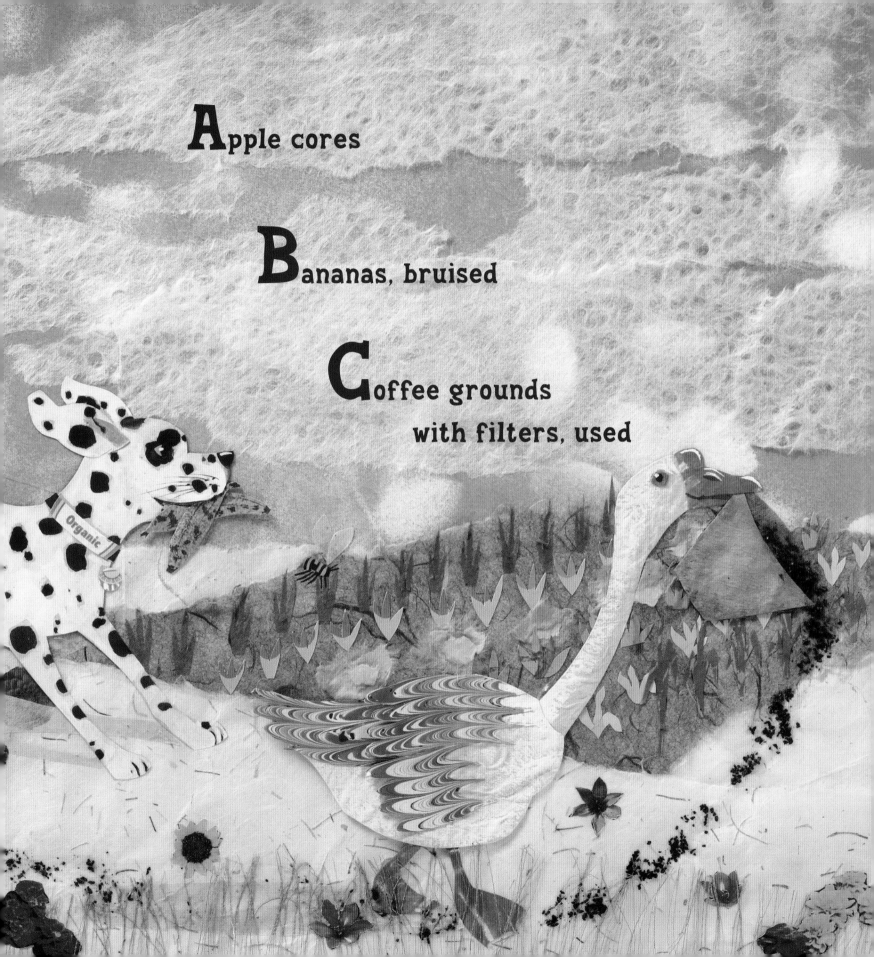

**A**pple cores

**B**ananas, bruised

**C**offee grounds
with filters, used

**D**irt clods, crumbled

**E**ggshells, crushed

**F**ruit pulp left behind, all mushed

**G**rass clippings

**H**air snippings

and an **I**nsect or two

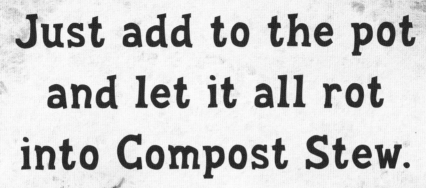

Just add to the pot
and let it all rot
into Compost Stew.

Save:

Jack-o'-lanterns

**K**itchen scraps

**L**aundry lint
from dryer traps

**M**ulch removed
from garden beds

**N**utshells

**O**atmeal

**P**aper shreds

Quarry dust

Rye bread crust

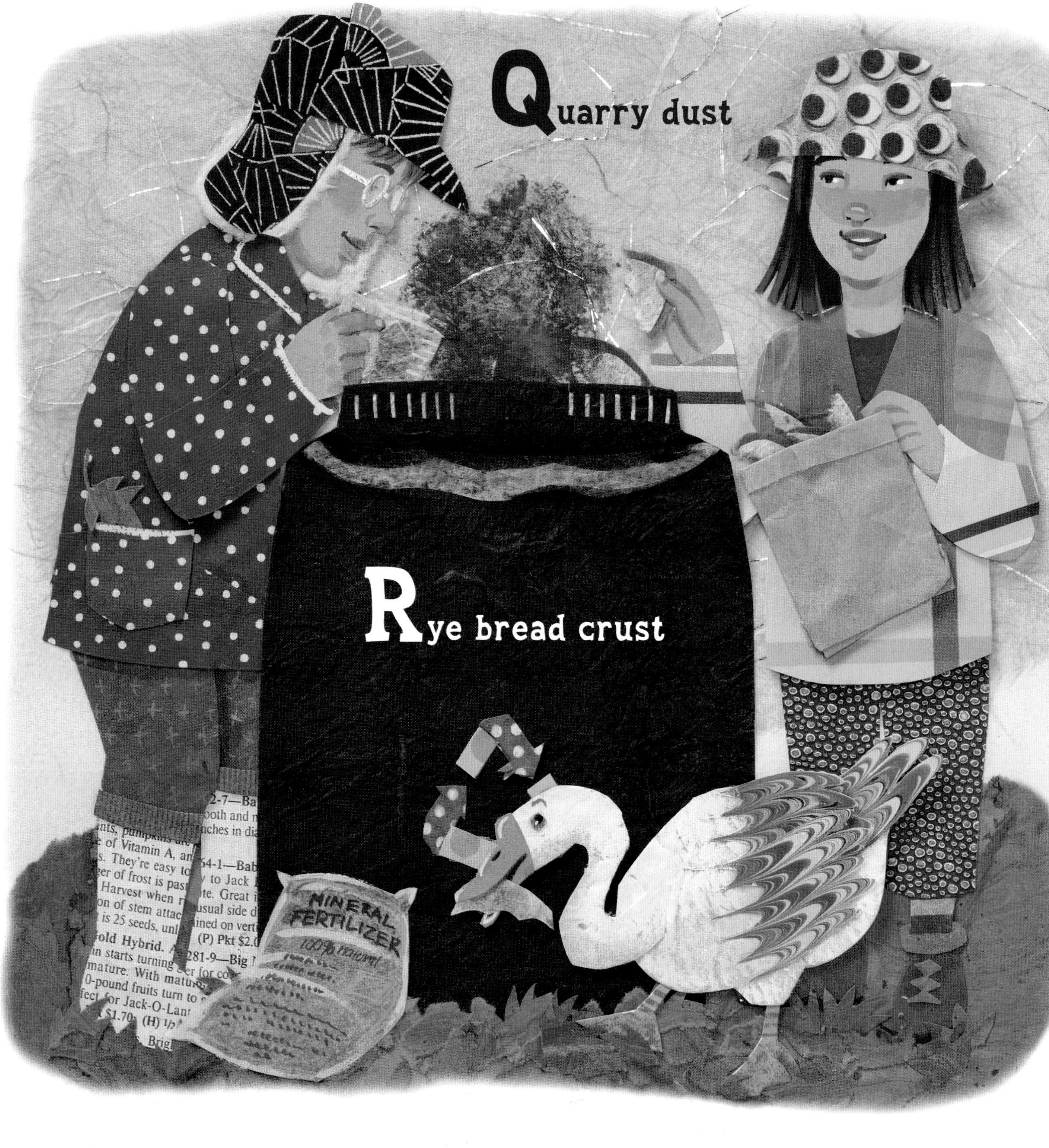

and **S**eaweed strands
(a few)

Just add to the pot
and let it all rot
into Compost Stew.

Take:

**T**eabags plucked from
long, hot swimmings

**U**nderbrush prunings

**V**egetable trimmings

# Wiggly worms with compost cravings

**X**mas tree needles

**Y**ellow pine shavings

and **Z**innia heads
from flower beds
whose blooming days are through

## Just add to the pot
## and let it all rot
## into Compost Stew.

**Moisten.**

**Toss lightly.**

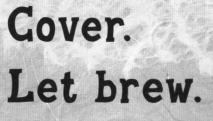

Cover.
Let brew.

And when the cooking
is complete,
Mother Earth will
have a treat,
dark and crumbly,
rich and sweet...

Now open the pot
and what have you got?

Compost Stew!

# Chef's Note

Out of pumpkins? Low on flies? Get creative! Improvise!
You can always substitute any veggie, plant, or fruit.

But please recycle these instead—they won't break down, so not a shred
of metal, plastic, packing foam, or chemicals found in the home.

What's more, no meat or dairy, please. No bones or gravy, fish or cheese,
for these will cause an awful smell, attracting animals as well.

Earthy? Yes! Meaty? No! Synthetic? Stop! Natural? Go!

So spice it up, but be judicious. Keep it wholesome and nutritious.
Mother Earth will say, "Delicious…Compost Stew!"

## Adapting the Recipe for Potluck Contributions
## (Or How to Keep Too Many Cooks from Spoiling the Stew):
Ingredients may vary from these general recommendations,
so whenever you've got a community pot, follow your local regulations.